I0531876

I (want to) love you, Baltimore

YELLOW ARROW PUBLISHING
WRITERS-IN-RESIDENCE

2022

I (want to) love you, Baltimore

Yellow Arrow Publishing

Annie Marhefka, Executive Director
Kapua Iao, Editor-in-Chief

with editorial associates
Sydney Alexander, Veronica Salib, and Rachel Vinyard

2022 Writers-in-Residence

Arao Ameny
Amy L. Bernstein
Catrice Greer
Matilda Young

cover photograph captured by Matilda Young

YELLOW ARROW
›› ———————→
PUBLISHING

Baltimore, MD
info@yellowarrowpublishing.com

We prioritize the unique voice and style of each of our authors.

Every writer has a story to tell and every story is worth telling.

Yellow Arrow Publishing

Table of Contents

Dear Readers,

In the spring of 2022, four Baltimore-based writers—Arao Ameny, Amy L. Bernstein, Catrice Greer, and Matilda Young—came together as a cohort during their writing residency program with Yellow Arrow Publishing. Each writer came with their unique story of how and why they wound up here, writing in Charm City, and they were challenged with the task of writing about their personal relationship with a very complicated, albeit enchanting, city.

As the four of them worked through their drafts, reading and sharing and offering the kindest and most constructive feedback and encouragement to one another, I had the great pleasure of facilitating. Through that process, I witnessed this collection's birth and growth. I marveled at how their poems inspired one another's words while still maintaining each writer's own voice and story, and I shared in as they reflected, laughed, cried, and celebrated together.

In one such session, Catrice shared a draft of her poem, "I Want to Love You, Baltimore" and for once, the virtual video chat line was silent at first. The rest of us then eagerly shared our love for the poem and its meanings, the way it resonated differently, hit home differently and the same, for each of us. It was immediately decided that this poem would be the titular poem of the collection, and the weeks that followed were filled with a reinvigorated fervor for writing.

I've often heard others marvel at how Baltimore's neighborhoods are not plotted out in a grid-like fashion, as in cities such as Chicago or nearby Washington, D.C. Rather, our streets feel almost happenstance, accidental. City blocks overlap like passengers packed into buses and each traveler's story presses itself upon us as we move through the streets. We are often encouraged to be intentional about our journeys, but sometimes wandering off course can lead to the most joyful encounters. In Baltimore, I have made some of the most charming discoveries and connections by just letting the city guide me—and often, by letting its artists guide me. Whether it is the lilt of a singer's voice escaping the windows of the local pub, a bold mural painted on the side of an old warehouse, or a spoken word performance at a community festival, artists enable us to view our city and our surroundings with fresh perspectives. Arao, Amy, Catrice, and Matilda have done this for me. Hearing their stories has added more depth and flavor to these spaces we share.

These writers were selected for the residency program based on their incredible writing talent and their desire to explore what Baltimore is to each of them, a journey that I think each of us works through when we ask what home means to us. I hope this collection will leave you contemplating what really divides and unites Charm City's neighborhoods.

Sincerely,

Annie Marhefka
Executive Director, Yellow Arrow Publishing

Annie Marhefka is a writer and publishing professional in Baltimore. Her creative nonfiction and poetry have been published by *Hobart*, *Literary Mama*, *Pithead Chapel*, *Anti-Heroin Chic*, *Sledgehammer*, and others. Annie is the executive director at Yellow Arrow and is working on a memoir about mother/daughter relationships. She spent the majority of her career as an executive in human resources in the ed-tech industry before switching paths to focus on motherhood and creative writing. When she's not writing or wrangling her children, she likes to spend her time on the Chesapeake Bay and other bodies of water. You can find Annie's writing on Instagram @anniemarhefka, Twitter @charmcityannie, and at anniemarhefka.com.

I (WANT TO) LOVE YOU, BALTIMORE

Mr. Trash Wheel
Matilda Young

In the shadow of the I-95 South ramp,
in an inlet of casino billboards & light
rail tracks, I watch Mr. Trash Wheel
lazily gobbling up detritus: a pink
Croc, a plastic bottle, a La Croix can,
a mask, a mask, a mask, a mask,
a mask. These days, I'm chasing comfort
on screens, baking competitions, drag
competitions, dating competitions,
wilds of Yorkshire, reboots on
reboots on reboots. I'm grabbing
at the last of happiness like I need to plug
it in, but I only have the charging
cord and not the block. But
I can keep my mouth open
to the river pouring in: folk hero trash
wheels, my first attempt at choux
pastry coming away from the side
of the pan, the angry cat curling
herself into my attempts at decoupage,
my friends huddling around a picnic
table at Peabody Heights, no one
wearing enough layers, everyone
trying to brazen it out, the MICA kid
with their easel painting a blurry pink
outline that could be open palm or fading
spirit or the Domino sign at dusk,
the young poet at the open mic who opens
with a song, his clear bass rising above
the slanting rooftops, calling us to sing

with him. I don't have to know
what's coming. I just have to taste it
all: shards, sun, Snapple, salt, wet salt.

Red Emma's Bookstore in Baltimore

Arao Ameny

is the only bookstore I went to
with an 'Africa' section

I meant to only stop for fifteen
minutes but three
hours later I wondered
where time had traveled

sometimes bookshelves welcome
immigrants more than people do
their aisles stretch and expand
wider than human hearts
And human minds
And human intentions
sometimes books
are the only saviors

so we read to belong
And we read for community
And we read to feel wanted
And we read to be part of something
And we read to remind ourselves
that we aren't foreign or different
or accented or accent-less
we read to become rooted
To become placed
To find refuge
To find refuge
To find refuge
To find refuge

I told my mother I like bookstores
more than I like people.

Nighttime Snapshot, with Jazz
Amy L. Bernstein

Down at the Keystone, a trio of cool horns warms the room lit with soft red lights, though the room is already warm because everybody who's there wants to be there, and nothing compares with the small emotional miracle of happiness that flares in your chest when the jazz is flowing, and heads are nodding to the backbeat and you and everyone around you can't stop smiling because the music feels so damn good. Is good. And that makes everything else a little bit better, at least for a moment.

*

The family of turtles living at the canal's dead-end a few blocks from the Keystone doesn't have a feel for jazz, but they do love to soak in the sun on their makeshift perch of a cage rocking atop the trash-infested ripples, the stone-enclosed remnant of old waterways and wharves that once jutted from the jam-end of petered out streets, everybody bustling, heading somewhere by land or by sea, except the turtles that show up with the season and don't have a mind to go anywhere except to the end of their natural little hard-shelled lives.

*

The girls in their slip dresses, goose-pimpled in the harbor-infused night air that's cooler than you'd hoped; those girls don't know about the turtles, but it's not their fault; they only come out after dark for negronis and espresso martinis at the so-called beach bar, which is really just a state of mind, and where the thumping metal bass beat would compete with the Keystone if they were a block closer together. The girls laugh and toss their hair and shift their weight from one stiletto heel to the other, wondering if maybe later they'll get pizza in Fell's Point.

*

The pack of teen boys in loose pants piloting scooters like bullet trains along the boardwalk are beneath the older girls' notice and the boys are concentrating on maximum warp, anyway, knowing the scooters aren't all that cool, but they're pretty cool when you really get going, when you get that weave and dip flowing, expertly grazing the air inches from a pedestrian's sneaker, an old woman's handbag. Going fast in the night, that's the cool part, and maybe terrorizing all the slow people a little, that's cool, too. And so is owning this piece of your city like a pro race car driver owns the track at Daytona. You take back a little of your own mojo each time you come out here.

*

'Round about midnight, the blue notes of the final trumpet solo slip out the door of the Keystone, on their way to flavor the harbor, caress the ears of couples slow-walking arm-in-arm to a nightcap or maybe to bed. White fiberglass motorboats with silly names emblazoned on the side—the *Tia Maria*, the *Aqua Vita*—bob on black waves, waiting for the fun to start up again. The scooter boys are long gone, dispersed to neighborhoods far from the water's reach, while the girls in slip dresses reapply a final swipe of lipstick after the last bite of pepperoni-mushroom-with-extra-mozzarella before tottering out into the cooling night, still open to possibilities.

Don't tell Ayaa that I'm in Baltimore

Arao Ameny

Don't tell my Ayaa that I'm in Baltimore
Don't tell my mother that I'm in Baltimore
Don't tell my Ayaa that I'm in Baltimore
Because she'll call me every morning to make sure I'm safe
And every night to make sure I'm alive
Don't tell my Ayaa she sold her belongings to come to America
So her daughter can live in this city
Don't tell her, my Ayaa

Tell Ayaa Zora Neal Hurston lives here
Tell Ayaa Edgar Allan Poe lives here
Tell Ayaa F. Scott Fitzgerald lives here
Tell Ayaa Lucille Clifton lives here.
Tell her, Ayaa, that the spirits who wrote
Some of her favorite books
Which I borrowed and became mine
Those spirits live here
They breathe here

Ayaa, are you listening?
You don't have to worry.
I write here.
I write here with them.
Don't worry, Ayaa.

(The letters immigrant daughters write to their mothers.)

All my Baltimore poems
are breakup poems these days.

Matilda Young

I met an incredible woman. She took me to trivia,
took me to meet her favorite tree, a small struggling
fir by a well-loved soccer field, brought me ginger
ale when the vaccine kicked my butt, ginger
chews when anxiety kicked my butt, watched
the sunrise with me over Fell's Point as the ducks
grumbled sleepily, her black hair brushing
my shoulder. We loved each other.
It didn't work out.

All my Baltimore poems are breakup poems these days.

I haven't been able to go back to Fell's Point or Patterson
Park or Roland Park or Canton Park or Druid Hill
Park without her—her unfiltered laughter, her bird IDs,
her warm hands holding my freezing ones.

All my Baltimore poems are breakup poems these days.

Look, I tell my broken heart, there's a sprawling,
messy, lovely city out there. Joggers in Reservoir Hill,
a kid with Crocs the color of courage, my old neighbor
from my last building with the square glasses
and the sweet, gray Scottie who still smiles and waves.

All my Baltimore poems are breakup poems these days.

There are millions of people here with their own sad
stories, families, tragedies, places they fell in love with,
with someone who's not coming back.

All my Baltimore poems are breakup poems these days.

I can love you, too, if you want

Arao Ameny

I am Baltimore
where Frederick Douglass learns
to read and write

I am the city
where Edgar Allan Poe's journey
begins and ends

I am Baltimore
where Zora Neale Hurston
also studies and grows

I can love you, too, if you want
I can love you, too, if you want

We write our disappointments to life

City of Crumbs

Amy L. Bernstein

The city is a layer cake
baking in thousands of ovens
set to varying temperatures
by bakers—alchemists all—
guarding family secrets scrawled
on batter-splattered index cards,

sacred texts for whipping up
a house, a home,
embroidered cushions on couches,
twin beds pushed against a window,
yards hosting splintered picnic tables
where cats spend their days mousing
while rainwater dribbles from a spout
into barrels feeding the garden

and families sit on front stoops
or lawn chairs splayed on sidewalks
waiting for the timer bell to ding

ding, ding, ding ding—
the tinny alarms echoing east, west,
north, south,
ricocheting off skyscraper walls . . .

Done!

And suddenly everyone in the city
is eating cake
at the same moment,
by the handful, the forkful,
lips and tongues all sugared up,

scent memories wafting along the avenues,
butter, sugar, cinnamon, chocolate, spices—
recipes like roadmaps to the future
of this layer cake city.

Kintsugi

Matilda Young

At an exhibit on Kyoto at the Met,
my young friend Alice told me
how artists will take broken
shards of porcelain, misfired,
fractured by table corners
and wrong footedness, and make
them whole again with lacquer
mixed with heated lines of gold.

Who am I then—in the story where
I stayed, commuting nowhere, still unfixed,
Baltimore with a window that opens
in grudging inches, aches that never go
away in that bad ankle on a cold hard
Tuesday at 3 am. Across from a parking
lot where the tow truck's lights gleam
in steady patterns, ambulances'
visitations, cypresses
baring themselves to December,
cartilage clacking in the cold.

At the Met, the gleaming stag stood
before us at the heart of the exhibit,
transformed into a messenger
whose element was mirrors, rows
of ornaments impossibly lit from within.
I wanted to run my hands
over the glass. I wanted to be
the person who believed in repair,
clean breakages.

I live alone, two blocks
from a park where children careen
on scooters and the dog owners
congregate with masks on and leashes
intertwined like macramé. One day,
one of the tiniest dogs broke toward
the street. I helped corral her.
She ran right into my arms.
I want to be a person who likes
themself. Some days, that's close
enough to true.

Back in New York, before we all shut
ourselves in, Alice told me about
the Israeli boy she met on Birthright,
how they just got each other, how maybe
she'd do the MFA, or maybe not.
I've known Alice since she was a perfect
toddler, and now she's twenty-four,
an artist, trying to figure it out. Sweet
as apple tart, good clean dirt,
flashes of gold, holding how we get
broken, how we, uneven, curious,
practice the art of being something
shattered, something new.

I Want to Love You, Baltimore

Catrice Greer

I want to see you,
want to see you win
want to see you grow

beyond your burrows, ports, redlines, black butterflies,
vacant homes, broken glass, and tattered flyers
waving goodbye to old memories and fractured neighborhoods.
Bring back the AFRO-Clean Block Revival
corner to corner

I want to see you
cherished like our historic Corned Beef Row

We are so political we can't see eye to eye and I lose you
in every election to a hope on the click of a switch

I want to see you and love you again,
roll in your Lake Roland grasses, unfold in your Cylburn gardens,
gathered in Druid Hill picnic memories
the fragrance of you, botanic

I want to see you, my love
can we grow together and find our way back from the rubble
of drawn lines hoarding wealth, starving city blocks
until they crack and bleed boarded vacancies and lack,
rampant water bills, lead paint, neglected properties, trampled rights,
housing issues, work inequities, respect lost, and just due

when I want to love you from the gutters as witness
I shake off the jewels of my privilege, your blind joy
from having so much, you disdain me for having so little
that to you it looks like overdue rent and sloth

to me, sometimes you look like the vacation, I've never had,
segregated in cul-de-sacs, time spent preening,
and my children's futures
slaving away the freedoms my ancestors bought
with blood and anonymity

I want to love you Baltimore
port to port
shore to shore
you elude me, you enchant me
we have so much to work out
and we will, in time,
we will

Choosing Home

Amy L. Bernstein

You might ask me
where I went to high school
or where I grew up,

and I'll reply, not here.

You might ask me who I root for—the Orioles, the Ravens, the Blast,
and I'll reply, none of the above.

You might ask me if I drink Natty Boh,
crunch Utz potato chips, and
lick the frosting off Berger's cookies

and you won't like my answer.

You might ask about
my favorite spot to crack crabs
slathered in Old Bay

and I'll tell you about the time I got
Old Bay in my eye.

You might ask me why the heck
I'm living in Baltimore, anyway?

And I'll climb up to the roof
and yell until I croak:

because of the way the sun glints on the Inner Harbor
at dusk as sailboats
make a lazy U, dodging kayaks.

Because of the way Cherry Hill is taking back its
own serpentine waterfront
along the Patapsco, one clump of weeds at a time.

Because of the way the old docks loom over the horizon
as you reach the top of Chester Street—ever a surprise.

The way the cherry blossoms explode in April on street corners
that were cold and forlorn five minutes earlier.

The way the old cobblestones bulge on the lanes of Fell's Point,
tripping the tipsy girls in heels.

The way a tiny rock-music palace sits next to an old dry cleaners.

Because of the way theaters take root in tired old warehouses,
the old warehouses brought back to life by brilliant
entrepreneurs in Pigtown.

The way the high school marching bands file along Pratt Street,
teenagers holding pom-poms doing back flips in the road
while some little guy bangs a drum twice his size.

The way the hordes of marathon runners take over the streets,
rendering cars useless, horns blaring, feet stomping.

The way Druid Hill Park rolls up over the city
with a big fat reservoir in the middle.

The way the city is filled with quiet pockets of old woods and
stone bridges,
if you know where to look.

Because of the way people tore down the enslavers' statues
in a righteous fit of justice.

The way all the community gardens carved from fallow lots
yield up tomatoes, lettuce, and squash in the heat of summer

while the farmers' markets do the rest, people shoulder to shoulder
picking over greens, standing in line for pickles and peas.

The way people in this city insist on living out loud in the present
with their Sunday finery and backyard bull roasts and rib feasts

while still grappling with a past that never leaves their side.
Our side.

I'll stand up here on the roof and tell you why I'm here
until the moon rises full, shedding her white light over the city
like a summer blanket.

You asked me so I'll tell you.

Baltimore is my home.
I have no other,
and cannot fathom why I should.

Meet the Writers

Arao Ameny is a Maryland-based poet and writer from Lango, Northern Uganda. She earned her MFA in creative writing in fiction at the University of Baltimore in 2019. She also earned an MA in journalism from Indiana University and a BA in political science from the University of Indianapolis. In 2020, her first published poem "Home is a Woman" appeared in *The Southern Review* and won the James Olney Award. In 2021, she was a winner of the Brooklyn Poets Fellowship, a finalist for the U.K.-based Brunel International African Poetry Prize, and a nominee for the U.S.-based Best New Poets anthology.

Amy L. Bernstein writes stories, essays, and poems that let readers feel while making them think. Her novels include *The Potrero Complex, The Nighthawkers, Dreams of Song Times*, and *Fran, The Second Time Around*. Poems have been published by *Yellow Arrow Journal, The Lark, Passaic-Voluspa, Loch Raven Review*, Lost Boys Press, *Parliament Literary Journal*, and elsewhere. Amy is an award-winning journalist, speechwriter, playwright, and certified nonfiction book coach. When not glued to a screen, she loves listening to jazz and classical music, drinking wine with friends, and exploring Baltimore's glorious neighborhoods, which inspire her writing. Learn more at amywrites.live.

Catrice Greer is a Baltimore-based writer and a 2021 Pushcart Prize nominee. In November 2020, she served as a Poet-In-Residence for Cheltenham Poetry Festival (U.K.). Her poetic work explores a range of topics about the human condition including mental health wellness, trauma, healing, sciences, nature, astronomy, transcendence, spirituality, identity, heritage, and cultural ancestry. She is published in local publications, online journals, and international anthologies. Currently, Catrice is co-editor of *Lapidus Magazine* (Bristol, U.K.), guest editor for IceFloe Press (Canada), and a guest poetry reviewer for Fevers of the Mind (U.S.).

Matilda Young is a poet with an MFA in poetry from the University of Maryland. She has been published in several journals, including *Anatolios Magazine, Angel City Review*, and *Entropy Magazine's* Blackcackle. She enjoys Edgar Allan Poe jokes, not being in her apartment, sharing viral birding videos, and being obnoxious about the benefits of stovetop popcorn. Follow Matilda on Instagram @matildayoung28.

Thank you for supporting independent publishing.

Yellow Arrow Publishing is a nonprofit supporting writers that identify as women. Visit YellowArrowPublishing.com for information on our publications, workshops, and writing opportunities.